This Book belongs to :

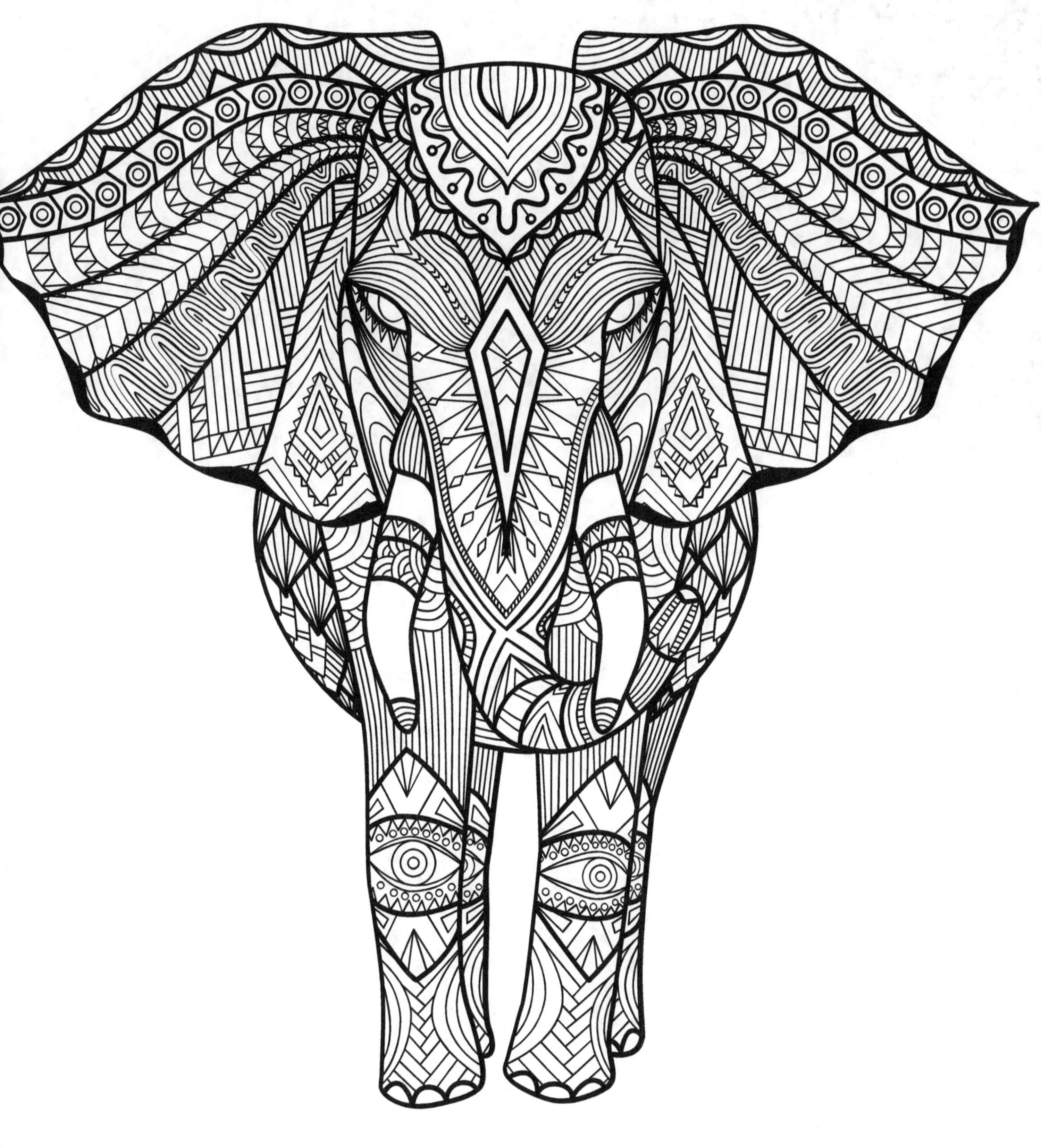

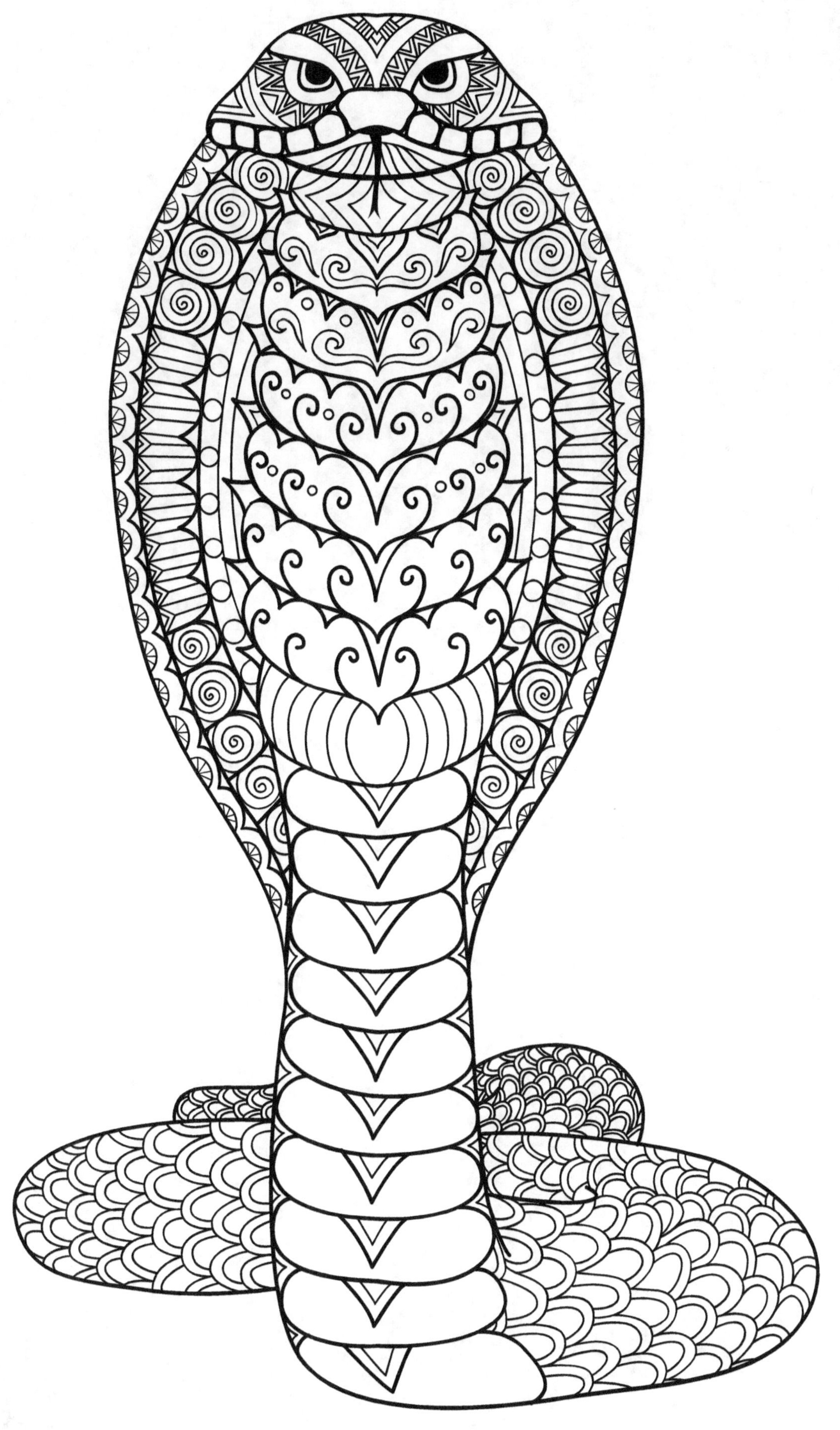

Thank you! 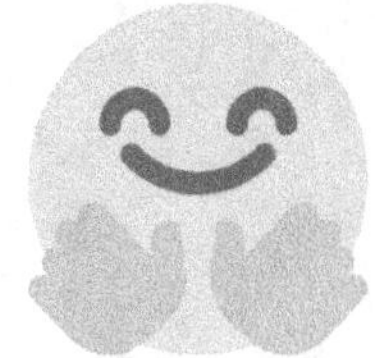

We hope you enjoyed our book. As a small family business, your feedback is very important to us.

Please let us know how you like our book at: Ampublishhing@gmail.com

Please check our book collection by scaning the QR code